Popular Chord Style Piano

by Robert Laughlin

Visit our website at pianofun.com

2 3 4 5 6 7 8 9 10 11 12 13 14 15

PT1101

Popular Chord Style Piano

SO YOU THINK YOU WANT TO PLAY THE PIANO

"If only I listened to my parents when I was younger. If only they <u>made</u> me practice the piano."

How many times we've heard that lament. Look, none of us needs yet another reason to blame our parents for anything they did or didn't do. The truth is, all the coaxing, cajoling, threatening, bribing, coercing, and pressuring in the world on the part of your parents would probably not have made a bit of difference anyway.

For one thing you want to play piano NOW. Back then you probably couldn't care less. For another thing, there's a 95% chance that even under the best of childhood circumstances, you wouldn't be playing piano today anyway.

But I've got some good news for you. First, if you can't play the piano now, it's not your fault. Second, it's not your parents' fault. And third, if you really want to learn piano as an adult, it's very easy to do. You can be playing your favorite songs in less than a week.

In fact, if you are taking the "Instant Piano for Hopelessly Busy People" seminar, you'll be playing all your favorite songs in less than four hours. But the seminar is intense. If you're using this book and audio program on your own, you'll probably want to take a more leisurely pace.

So we're going to give you one week.

But wait a minute. Doesn't this fly in the face of everything you've heard about piano lessons? Yes it does, I suppose. Understand our method is different to be sure. Numerous myths surround the piano learning process. In this course we'll dispel these myths and give you a fresh look at an old instrument.

Myth 1: You have to be a good note reader to play an instrument.

Fact: This is true if you are playing classical music only. But a great many pop piano players (and damn good ones at that) don't read a single note of music. You're going to learn their method. It's the preferred method for nonclassical players.

What to Practice at This Point

Be absolutely certain to use the accompanying audio program as a guide to the following topics.

1. C and G chords
    a. Strive for a quick, smooth change.
    b. Hand is relaxed, fingers slightly curved.

2. Lightly Row: Combine both hands
    a. Keep the measures of consistent duration.
    b. Play as slowly as you need.
    c. Tap your left foot and count to four.

3. Arpeggios
    a. Practice on C, F, and G chords.
    b. Start slowly, gradually increase speed.
    c. Keep it smooth and steady. Don't sacrifice precision for speed.
    d. Left hand crosses over the right. Right hand pulls out from under left.
    e. Put in context of Lightly Row.
        (as demonstrated on audio program)

4. Chromatic Major Chord Scale
    a. Practice it without reading the music.
    b. Practice it in both directions.
    c. Start with left hand only. Then right only. Then both together.
    d. The Ultimate challenge: Eyes closed.

MORE SONGS

The following songs have been selected to prepare you for playing any popular song. We will be looking at different key signatures, different time signatures, and other features of written music such as ties, accidentals, pick-up notes, and multiple chord patterns. The idea is to practice these tunes until they sound just like they do on the audio program. Then apply this knowledge to music of your own choosing. If you don't already have your own music to play, get some. Any songs will do as long as they are written out with chord symbols to follow, they are familiar to you, and they are songs that you want to learn to play.

Song Example 2: Marianne

Topics Covered in Audio Program:
1. How to approach learning a new song
2. How to interpret the tie

Marianne

Song Example 3: Tom Dooley

Topics Covered in Audio Program:

1. Introduces the dominant seventh chord
2. Learn to use the chord chart
3. On learning new chords (write them in the music)
4. Key signature
    a. What it is
    b. Why is it important?
    c. What is not important about it?
    d. Simple way to identify key signatures
    e. How does key signature affect chords?
5. Dealing with rhythm (counting) in the melody

7th - 1 whole step down from root.

add a grace note

add filler notes

C 5
A 3
F# 2
D 1

Tom Dooley

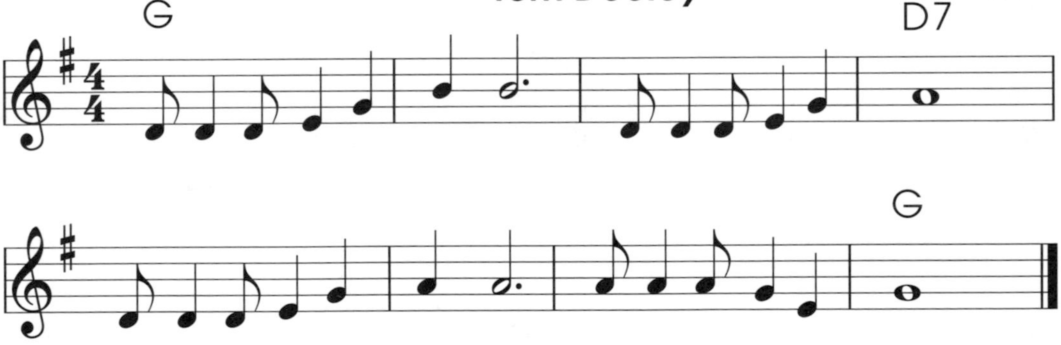

Three ways to look up chords:

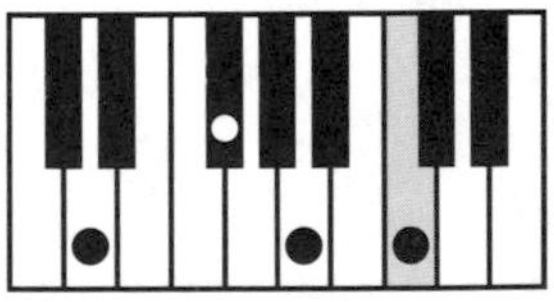

for beginners

for intermediates

for advanced

Song Example 4:   Down In The Valley

Topics Covered in Audio Program:
     1. Two new chords (be sure to spell them out as in the previous example)
     2. New key signature
          a. What it means to the right hand
          b. What it is called
     3. New time signature
     4. How to handle any time signature
          a. Look at top number only
          b. One exception to this rule

right hand

- grace notes
- octaves
- add chord tones

Down In The Valley

The Key Signature

    A sharp sign on the top F line of the staff means all the F's in the melody of the song are played as F-sharp. Likewise the sharp sign on the C space of the staff means all C's in the melody are to be played as C-sharps. In this example there are two of each.

    Key signatures do not affect the chord symbols. If there were a C chord in the song, it would be played as a C chord, not a C-sharp chord.

Song Example 5: Joshua Fit The Battle Of Jericho

Topics Covered in Audio Program:
1. Minor chords
    a. Look up the Dm chord
    b. Learn to recognize its distinctive sound
2. Minor key signature
    a. When the first and last chords of a song are minor, the song is said to be in a minor key
    b. This gives the entire song a minor flavor
    c. Minor chords can also be found in songs that are in major keys
3. Accidentals
    a. They last for a full measure
    b. Key signatures are permanent
4. Special time signature 2/2
    a. Play it as if it were 4/4
    b. Usually indicates a faster tempo (speed)
5. Rhythmic freedom of interpretation

chord pulsing

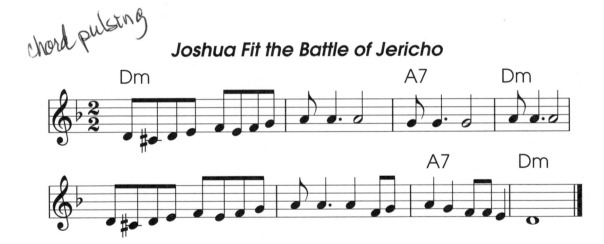

Joshua Fit the Battle of Jericho

The B-flat in the key signature means every B note in the melody is to be changed to B-flat. Except in this song there are none.

The upper digit in a time signature indicates the number of beats to count in a measure. The exception is if the time signature is 2/2 as it is here. Then it means to count four beats.

The C-sharp in the first measure is an accidental. Any other C's in the first measure then would also have to be converted to C-sharp. Except here there are none.

Song Example 6:   When The Saints Go Marching In

Topics Covered in Audio Program:
1. Three chord song
2. Pick-up notes
3. Syncopation
4. Dissonance

When The Saints Go Marching In

Popular Chord Style Piano

Song Example 7:   The Entertainer

Topics Covered in Audio Program:
    1. Learning a difficult song
    2. Special problems
        a. Many chords
        b. Two chords per measure
        c. Syncopation
        d. Difficult right hand rhythm

Procedure:
    1. Master the left hand part first
        a. Memorize all the chords (six of them)
        b. Practice playing these chords in proper sequence
        c. Practice this chord progression using the correct rhythm
            1) Two chords per measure
            2) Left hand must keep steady rhythm (beat)
            3) Count four beats (or foot taps) per measure
            4) Chords are played on beats "one" and "three"
        d. Must add chords to beat "three" of some measures
        e. LEARN LEFT HAND PERFECTLY BEFORE ADDING RIGHT HAND
    2. Then add the right hand
        a. Chord symbols line up with melody notes
        b. Play both hands very slowly at first (keeping beat steady)
        c. Gradually increase speed

The Entertainer

By Scott Joplin

DERIVING MINOR AND SEVENTH CHORDS

Minor Chords

To change a major chord to a minor chord just lower the middle note of the major chord one half-step. In other words, shift the middle note of the major chord one note to the left.

	G		G
Thus, the C major chord is	E	and the C minor chord is	Eb
	C		C

The Twelve Major Chords

C   Db   D   Eb   E   F   Gb   G   Ab   A   Bb   B

The Twelve Minor Chords

Cm   Dbm   Dm   Ebm   Em   Fm   Gbm   Gm   Abm   Am   Bbm   Bm

Seventh Chords

To change a major chord to a seventh chord you add a fourth note to it. The note you add is one whole-step (two half-steps) below the root. In other words 1) locate the root, 2) locate the note that lies two notes to the left of the root, 3) add this note to the chord only one octave higher.

The seventh chord will sound better if you place this extra note at the top of the chord, leaving the root at the bottom. This is a C seventh chord:

Bb
G
E
C

The Twelve Seventh Chords

C7   Db7   D7   Eb7   E7   F7   Gb7   G7   Ab7   A7   Bb7   B7

THE CHORD SIMPLIFICATION FLOW CHART

major seventh - down 1 half step from root

There are several thousand different chords that can be played on the piano. That's the bad news. The good news is that (with a couple of rather insignificant exceptions) these chords all fall into one of three general categories: major, minor, or seventh. This means that you don't have to learn thousands of different chords. You will be able to get by for a long time by using only the thirty-six chords that you have already learned. The trick is to substitute one of these thirty-six chords for any advanced chord you may encounter in your music. The only problem is knowing which type of chord to substitute--major, minor, or seventh. The flow chart will provide the answer to this problem. Here's how it works.

Whenever you encounter an unfamiliar chord, answer the first question you come to in the chart: "Does the chord have a single 'm' in it?" From there you answer the questions and follow the appropriate arrows until the chart finally leads you to the correct substitution either major, minor, or seventh.

Please be aware, however, that complex chords can add beautiful tonal colors to your music. When you simplify chords you take away these subtle colors even though the simplified chords sound correct. Thus, you should think of chord simplification as merely a temporary strategy. Use it so you can play all your favorite songs as soon as possible. Eventually you will want to learn to play the chords the way the composer intended.

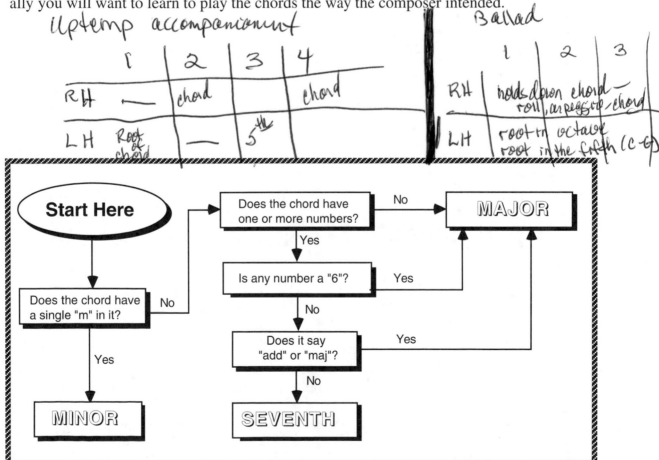

This flow chart works for all chord types except augmented and diminished.

Complete Chord Chart

These are the thirty-six chords you need to know. With them you will be able to play any song in any key. Feel free to read them either in the treble clef or the bass clef. They are the same either way. If you read them from the treble clef, remember to play them with the left hand and one full octave below the way they are written. If you read them from the bass clef, play them as written.

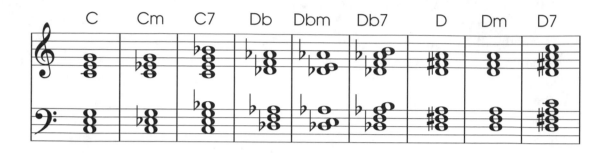

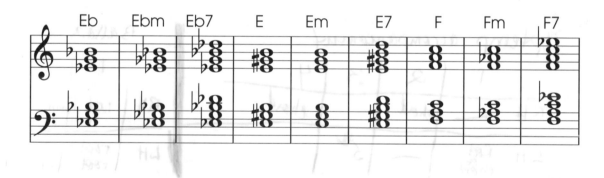

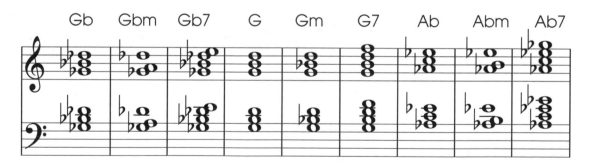

Chord Diagrams Complete

The Major Group

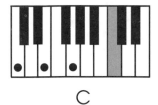

C

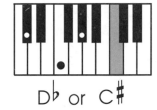

D♭ or C#

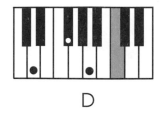

D

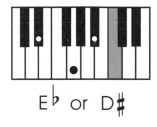

E♭ or D#

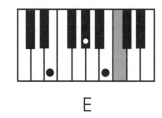

E

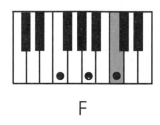

F

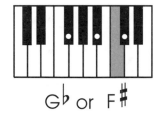

G♭ or F#

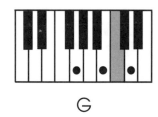

G

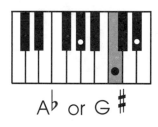

A♭ or G#

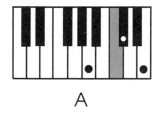

A

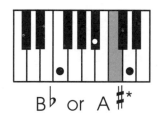

B♭ or A#*

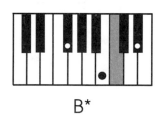

B*

The Minor Group

Cm

D♭m or C♯m

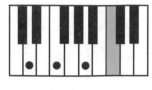

Dm

E♭m or D♯m

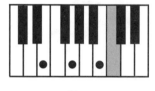

Em

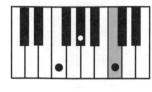

Fm

G♭m or F♯m

Gm

A♭m or G♯m

Am

B♭m or A♯m*

Bm*

Popular Chord Style Piano

The Seventh Group

C7*

D♭7 or C#7

D7

E♭7 or D#7

E7

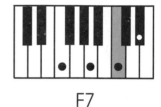

F7

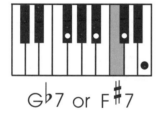

G♭7 or F#7

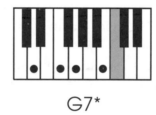

G7*

A♭7 or G#7*

A7*

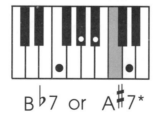

B♭7 or A#7*

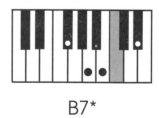

B7*

Shaded note represents middle C. Play chords with the left hand as shown in these diagrams. An asterisk denotes chord is in an inverted form. An inverted chord is one whose notes are rearranged so the chord's root is no longer the bottom (lowest sounding) note.

FINAL WORDS

Practice

Practice is vital. You won't improve without it, so try to do some playing every day. There's much to be said for a strict practicing regimen that includes scales and exercises, but not everyone enjoys playing scales and exercises. Strive to make your piano playing a pleasant experience. The very word "practice" has a negative connotation. So don't practice. Play. "Play" is a much better word.

While it's true that you will only improve if you practice, you will only practice if you enjoy doing it. If you enjoy practicing scales and exercises, fine. However, if you only enjoy playing music, that's what you should be doing. Have fun with the songs, and don't feel guilty. Practice should be a pleasurable activity, and it's up to you to keep it pleasurable.

Next

This course is designed to give you the basic tools for pop piano playing. You will want to work with these tools until they become second nature to you. Now that you've learned these piano basics, you may want to start expanding your knowledge of the piano right away. The more you know, the more enjoyable it is to play. The more enjoyable it is to play, the more playing you will do. The more playing you do, the better you get.

Additional courses to supplement this one are listed on the last page. Once you grasp the concepts of using chords, consider yourself ready for any of them.

Glossary

Accidentals - Melody notes that are modified by sharp, flat, or natural signs. As such they do <u>not</u> occur naturally in the scale of the key signature. When placed before a note in music notation the accidental raises or lowers the pitch of that note by a half step. An accidental is valid for one whole measure.

Accompaniment Style - A method of piano playing which emphasizes a song's chords and is employed primarily when the song's melody is sung or played by another instrument. See also *solo style*.

Bar Line - Vertical lines in music notation which divide music into *measures*.

Bass - Pertains to lower pitched tones.

Beat - A single unit of the steady pulse that occurs throughout a song. There are always the same number of beats in every measure within a given song

Chord - Three or more notes played simultaneously. An omnipresent and vital part of all music. See also *harmony*.

Chord Changes - The specific sequence of chords occurring throughout a piece of music. Also referred to as *chord progression* and *chord structure*.

Double Bar - In music notation two short, parallel lines of unequal thickness which indicate a song is over.

Flat Sign - The symbol ♭ which indicates a note is to be played one half step lower than written. Generally lowers a white note to a black note.

Half Step - The shortest distance (interval) in music. Equivalent to any two adjacent keys (including the black keys) on the keyboard.

Harmony - Notes which support the melody of a song. Used interchangeably with *chord progression*.

Interval - Term used to describe the distance between notes in music.

Inversion - The particular order from bottom to top in which the individual notes of a chord are played.

Key - That particular scale or set of notes around which a song is based.

Key Signature - The collection of sharp signs or flat signs grouped at the beginning of each line of music. Indicates the key the song is in, and reveals which black notes are most likely to be found in a song's melody and its chord progression.

Major - One of many classifications of chords. There are 12 chords associated with each classification.

Measure - A unit of time in music indicated by bar lines. All measures in the same song are usually of equal duration.

Melody - A sequence of single notes that is either sung or played by one or more instruments. It is perhaps the most prominent feature of a piece of music.

Minor - One of many classifications of chords. There are 12 chords associated with each classification.

Musician's Notation - Similar to Regular Classical Music Notation, only it's simpler. The chord symbols are placed above the staff, and there may or may not be a melody indicated.

Natural Sign - The symbol ♮ indicates a note is to be played on the natural white key where it would otherwise be played as a black key by virtue of an accidental or a key signature.

Pickup Measure - The first measure of some songs that contain one or more melody notes but no chord symbols. The pickup measure always lacks the correct number of beats.

Pickup Notes - The melody notes in a pickup measure.

Pitch - Indicates whether a note is high or low.

Popular Music - For our purposes, all music that isn't classical.

Root - That particular note within a chord that has the same name as the chord itself. All chords have a root.

Root Position - That particular inversion of a chord where the root is the lowest note of the chord.

Scale - A sequence of notes, unique to each key, from which the majority of a song's melody notes and chord notes are taken.

Seventh - One of many classifications of chords. There are 12 chords associated with each classification.

Sharp Sign - The symbol ♯ which indicates a note is to be played one half step higher than written. Generally raises a white note to a black note.

Slur - A curved line in music notation which indicates a syllable of a song's lyrics is shared among two or more melody notes.

Solo Style - A method of piano playing which combines a song's melody with its chords and is employed primarily when the piano playing stands alone (without singing). See also *accompaniment style*.

Tempo - The speed at which a piece of music is played.

Tie - A curved line in music notation (similar to a slur) which joins two or more separately written notes into one single note held for the duration of the tie.

Time Signature - A symbol found at the beginning of the first line of a song, consisting of two numbers, one above the other. It indicates how many beats occur in each measure.

Transpose - To change the key in which a song is written.

Additional Resources

Blues Piano Styles (two cassettes, workbook)

If you want to create bluesy piano sounds, get this course immediately. Virtually no other piano teacher will <u>ever</u> teach you the incredibly versatile blues scale—or any of the other blues devices found in this volume. The time is NOW to start working on the basics of blues rhythm and harmony. It's simple, and it's fun. Includes basic Blues/Boogie cassette and Blues Improvising cassette. All levels.

ISBN 0-929983-11-4

Continuing Chord Piano (four cassettes, workbook, vinyl album)

Picks up where *Popular Chord Style Piano* leaves off. Reveals some of the best playing techniques and tricks of the pros (many of which are closely guarded secrets). Most are adaptable to the blues and will turbo charge your playing. One cassette for left hand variations, one for right hand variations, and two cassettes of chord drills. It's the perfect pump-up for beginning pop and blues piano players who are ready to shatter the barriers of mediocre playing. Beginning to intermediate.   ISBN 0-929983-16-5

How to Play Piano by Ear (five cassettes, workbook, vinyl album)

What if your sheet music doesn't have the chord symbols? What if you want to learn a hard-to-find song from a recording? You're stuck, right? Wrong. Not if you have the *Piano by Ear Course*. It's exactly the same workshop that has taught thousands of tin ears the secret of faking it with style. Results guaranteed. All levels (but you should know your chords first).   ISBN 0-929983-02-5

Power Chords/Intros and Endings (two cassettes, two workbooks)

These two courses work together to provide a more advanced follow-up to *Continuing Chord Piano*. *Power Chords* gives fresh alternatives to the basic chords you already know. Explains inversions and voicings too. Great for giving old songs new life. *Intros and Endings* enables you to embellish songs even further with up-to-date, professional sounding introductions and endings. Both programs are geared to all forms of popular music, and the tricks and ideas you learn will enhance your playing. Intermediate to advanced level.

Power Chords :   ISBN 0-929983-13-0
Intros and Endings: ISBN 0-929983-14-9

Praise! (cassette, workbook)

A super easy introduction to chord piano playing, using well known hymns and inspirational songs. As it uses only the chords necessary for playing the songs, it's an excellent introductory piano course. Also introduces the art of piano accompaniment. Easy level.   ISBN 0-929983-19-X

The Season (two cassettes, workbook)

A collection of sixteen all-time favorite Christmas Carols, complete with learning guide. An excellent resource for learning new songs, chords, and keys. You won't find a more delightful way to learn. Optional tapes teach how to arrange selected carols, and provide dozens of ideas for further improvisation. Easy to intermediate.   ISBN 0-929983-22-X

Piano Tricks & Licks (one cassette)

Enhance your playing with new ideas and fresh inspiration. A well balanced presentation of exercises, chord substitutions, music theory, stylings, and a healthy dose of piano player's "cheap tricks" sharpens skills and improves sound. It's like having a pro player in your own home giving you a private lesson! Intermediate.   ISBN 0-929983-04-1

Blatantly Basic Blues (one video cassette)

Now we have a video to add to our acclaimed audio programs. Two cameras mean two simultaneous keyboard angles, allowing you to both see and hear the examples as they are played. Acquaints you with all the blues basics of form, chords, and scales, then goes much deeper into improvising and the styles of Professor Longhair, Fats Domino, and Ray Charles. Beginning through intermediate. ISBN 0-929983-23-8

Note: These titles, as well as live workshops, are available through Workshop Leaders trained in the Laughlin Method. For the name of the certified Workshop Leader nearest you, call 530-872-7664 or visit our website: www.pianofun.com.

NOTES

This land is your land

This land is my land

From California to the NY Island

From the redwood forest

To the gulf stream waters

This land was made for you & me